EXPERIMENTS WITH WATER

A TRUE BOOK

by

Salvatore Tocci

Children's Press®

A Division of Scholastic Inc.

New York Toronto London Auckland Sydney
Mexico City New Delhi Hong Kong
Danbury, Connecticut

Reading Consultant
Nanci R. Vargus, Ed.D
Primary Multiage Teacher
Decatur Township Schools
Indianapolis, Indiana

Science Consultant
Robert Gardner

The author and publisher are
not responsible for injuries or accidents
that occur during or from any
experiments. Experiments should be
conducted in the presence of or with the
help of an adult. Any instructions of the
experiments that require the use of
sharp, hot, or other unsafe items should
be conducted by or with the
help of an adult.

Library of Congress Cataloging-in-Publication Data

Tocci, Salvatore.
Experiments with water / Salvatore Tocci.
     p.   cm. – (A True book)
  Includes bibliographical references and index.
  ISBN 0-516-22508-1 (lib. bdg.)   0-516-26996-8 (pbk.)
  Water–Experiments—Juvenile literature. [1. Water—Experiments.
2. Experiments.] I. Title. II. Series.

GB662.3 .T63 2001
546'.22'078—dc21   00-069382

Contents

How Hot Can It Get?

What do you think of when you hear the word desert? You probably imagine a large, sandy area where it can get very hot. Death Valley in California is such a place.

Death Valley is the hottest place in North America. The average high temperature during the summer is around 115°F (46°C). During the winter, however, the temperature can drop to zero. It was during the winter of 1849 when a group of pioneers became the first people to cross Death Valley.

These pioneers were looking for a new route from Utah to California where gold had just been discovered. While crossing the desert, the pioneers ran out of food. To eat, they had to kill the oxen that pulled their wagons. There was something

In a desert, a spot where water can usually be found is called an oasis.

else that the pioneers needed to survive. Fortunately, they found what they needed in Death Valley. What the pioneers found was water.

Where Do We Get Our Drinking Water?

The pioneers had been crossing the desert for almost a month when their supply of water was about to run out. They were saved by a snowstorm. The pioneers melted the snow to get the drinking water that they needed to survive. They then continued on their journey across Death Valley.

Today scientists know that snow melting into water is part of the water cycle. In this cycle, water is constantly passed back and forth, or recycled, between different places in nature. Is there a way to see how water is recycled in nature?

Recycling Water

You will need:
- large, wide-mouth glass jar with screw-on lid
- small rocks
- sand
- soil
- two small plants
- cap from a liquid laundry detergent container

Cover the bottom of the jar with small rocks. Then add a layer of sand. Cover the sand with a layer of soil. Place the plants in the soil. Fill the cap with water and place it on the soil. Screw on the lid and place the jar in a sunny spot for several days. How much water is there in the cap?

This jar is a model of how the water cycle operates in nature.

Do you see water droplets on the inside surface of the jar?

The sun heats up the water in the cap. When the water gets hot enough, it turns into a gas that evaporates into the air. This gas is commonly called steam. Scientists call it water vapor.

Inside the jar, the water vapor collects on the glass. The glass cools the vapor, turning it back into water. This water may fall back into the cap. The sun again heats up the water in the cap. The water turns into vapor that again collects on the glass.

Water turns into steam when it boils.

Water can be recycled between the bottle cap and the glass surface.

The vapor on the glass can also drip onto the soil inside the jar, where it slowly seeps into the soil. The roots of the plants absorb the water. The plants use some of this water. The rest of the water is released by the leaves as vapor. The vapor collects on the glass. The vapor is then cooled and turns back into water. The water can drip into the cap or onto the soil. Inside the jar, water is being recycled between the soil, plants, cap, and glass.

Use your finger to follow how water travels from the bottle cap, to the glass, to the soil, to the plant, and finally back to the glass. As the vapor cools on the glass, where can the water go?

What happens in the jar is a model of what happens in nature.

Think of the cap as an ocean, lake, river, or pond. The sun turns the water into vapor. Think of the glass as the sky. The vapor rises from Earth into the sky, where it forms clouds. When the vapor in a cloud cools, it turns into precipitation, such as rain or snow. This precipitation can wind up in the ocean or some other body of water. This water can again be heated by the sun and turn into vapor. This vapor again rises into the sky to form new clouds. This is part of the water cycle.

13

Use your finger to follow how water travels from the pond, to the sky, to the land, to the trees, and finally back to the sky. As the vapor cools in the clouds, where can the water go?

Precipitation can also fall on land. The rain or melted snow can seep into the ground. This water is known as groundwater. Plants absorb groundwater. Plants release most of this water back into the air as vapor. This vapor rises into the air to form new clouds and continue the water cycle.

After two months in the desert, the pioneers in Death Valley found an underground spring that provided all the water they needed. Like these pioneers, most people in the United States today get their drinking water from underground.

Remember that groundwater comes from precipitation that seeps down through the soil. The soil filters the water, making it safe to drink. However, the soil cannot filter out everything that gets into the ground. As a result, the groundwater supply in many areas is becoming polluted. Some of this pollution is caused by fuel that leaks from storage tanks and gets into the water supply. Chemicals that are spread on the ground can also pollute groundwater. These

The chemicals in fuel leaking from rusted tanks and in pesticides can pollute the groundwater.

chemicals include fertilizers and pesticides that are applied to lawns and crops. You can make a model of groundwater pollution just as you did of the water cycle.

Experiment 2

Polluting Water

You will need:
- scissors
- nylon mesh (available at a hardware store)
- thick marker
- plastic tie
- two large paper cups
- potting soil
- plastic spoon
- sand
- food coloring
- dropper

Cut the nylon mesh to get a piece large enough to wrap around the marker. Wrap the nylon piece around the marker. Use the plastic tie to hold the nylon mesh around the marker. Hold the nylon-wrapped marker with one hand in the middle of a paper cup. Use your other hand to pour in enough of the potting soil to fill the cup and surround the nylon-wrapped marker. Remove the plastic tie from the marker. Carefully slide the marker out of the nylon mesh. The mesh should remain in the cup.

Fill the other paper cup with water. Add several spoonfuls of sand and ten drops of food coloring. Mix everything well. Slowly pour some of this colored sand-water mixture into the soil surrounding the nylon mesh. Be sure not to pour any of this mixture inside the nylon mesh. Wait about ten minutes. Use the dropper to remove some water from inside the nylon mesh. How does this water look?

The nylon mesh acts as a well. The surrounding soil filters the water that you poured into the cup. The soil keeps the sand from getting into the water inside the mesh. However, the soil cannot keep the food coloring from getting into the water. The food coloring acts like a chemical that can get into a well and pollute the groundwater.

Like the pioneers in the desert, lots of people have found themselves in need of water. Unlike the pioneers, however, many of these people were actually surrounded

People stranded in the ocean should not drink the salt water, no matter how thirsty they are.

by water but they could not drink it. These people were on the ocean. The salts in ocean water make it unhealthy to drink. Is there a way to turn salt water into drinking water?

21

Making Drinking Water

You will need:
- small glass bowl
- large bowl
- large measuring cup
- salt
- spoon
- plastic wrap
- modeling clay

Place the small bowl in the middle of the large bowl. Fill the measuring cup with water. Add several spoonfuls of salt and stir. Pour this salt water into the large bowl. Be careful not to get any salt water into the small bowl. Cover the bowls with plastic wrap. Place a weight such as a small ball of clay on the middle of the plastic wrap. Leave the bowls in the sun for several days.

Notice the water droplets that collect on the plastic wrap. The weight on the plastic wrap causes these droplets to fall into the small bowl. Remove the plastic wrap. Use your

22

finger to taste the water in the small bowl. Does this water taste salty?

Heat from the sun evaporates the water in the large bowl. The vapor rises and lands on the plastic wrap. The plastic wrap cools the vapor and turns it back into water. This water then drips into the small bowl. The salts in the water, however, do not evaporate. The salts remain behind in the large bowl. You have turned salt water from the large bowl into drinking water in the small bowl.

If you do not have any clay, you can use anything that will weigh down the plastic wrap so that it sinks in the middle.

What Does Water Do?

The pioneers could have lived without food for over a month but without water, they would have died in less than a week. The body needs water to carry out all the work it does. Humans are not alone in needing water to survive. All living things need water to survive. What else does water do besides keeping things alive?

Experiment 4

Floating on Water

You will need:
• large bowl
• modeling clay
• marbles

Fill the bowl with water. Roll a piece of modeling clay into a ball. Place the clay ball on top of the water. Then place some marbles on top of the water. What happens to the clay ball and marbles?

Remove the clay ball and marbles from the water. Shape the clay so that it looks like a boat. Place the clay boat on top of the water. The clay boat should float. Place the marbles, one at a time, into the clay boat. The boat should sink lower into the water, but it should still float.

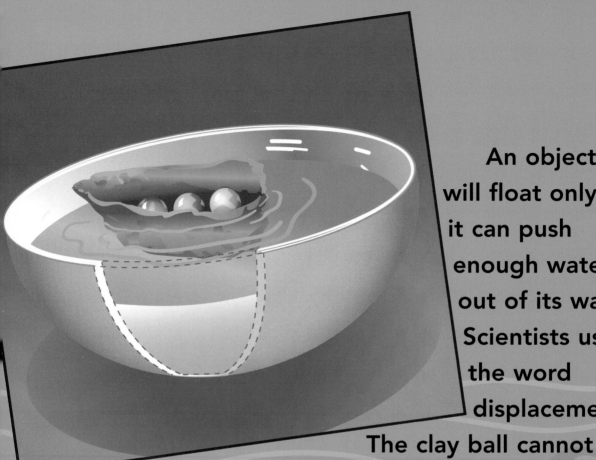

An object will float only if it can push enough water out of its way. Scientists use the word displacement. The clay ball cannot displace enough water to float—neither can the marble. So they sink. The clay boat has a different shape than the clay ball. Because of its shape, the clay boat can displace enough water to float. The water inside the bowl pushes up on the clay boat. So the boat floats, even when you add the marbles.

Some things must be able to float some of the time and sink at other times. For example, a submarine must be able to move along the surface of the water and also dive deep into it. How does a submarine do this?

Moving Up and Down

You will need:
- modeling clay
- plastic top from a pen
- tall drinking glass
- tall, clear plastic bottle with a screw-on lid

Shape a piece of clay into a tiny ball. Then stick the ball on the sharp point of the pen cap. Fill the glass with water. Put the pen top into the water. If the pen top sinks, remove some of the clay from the ball. If the pen top does not stand straight up, add some more clay. You want the pen top and clay to float straight up in the water. Completely fill the plastic bottle with water. Put the pen top in the bottle. Screw the lid on tightly. Squeeze the middle of the bottle very

The clay ball must be just the right size so that the pen top floats straight up and down in the water.

hard. What happens to the pen top? Let go of the bottle. Now what happens to the pen top? When you squeeze the bottle, you force water into the pen top. The pen top gets heavier and sinks. When you let go, the water rushes out of the pen top. This makes the pen top lighter, and it rises to the surface. Submarines have special tanks that can be flooded with water. The submarine gets heavier and can dive beneath the surface. To come back to the surface, air is pumped into these tanks to force the water back out into the sea. The submarine gets lighter and can then float to the surface.

What Is So Unusual About Water?

The pioneers were lucky to find water in Death Valley. The desert is one of the few spots on Earth where there is little water. In fact, more than 70 percent of the Earth is covered with water. Most of this water is in the oceans. Water also makes

The amount of water in this girl's body is the same as the amount of water in these buckets.

up the biggest part of many living things. For example, water makes up about 65 percent of the human body.

Water is not only very common, it is also very unusual. For one thing, water is the only substance on Earth that can be found easily in three different forms. You can find it as a liquid from a faucet, as a solid (ice) in a freezer, and as a gas (vapor) coming from boiling water in a tea kettle. What else is unusual about water?

Sticking Together

You will need:
- bowl
- small paper clips
- fork
- liquid detergent
- large spoon

Fill the bowl with water. Gently rub a paper clip across your forehead. This will transfer a little of the grease from your forehead to the paper clip. The grease will prevent water from sticking to the paper clip. Gently lower the paper clip onto the water with a fork.

Lower the paper clip slowly or else it will sink.

Lower another paper clip onto the water. How many paper clips can you get to float on the water?

Remove the paper clips from the water. Add a few drops of liquid detergent to the water. Use the spoon to mix the detergent and water. Stir gently to avoid making suds. Now see how many paper clips you can get to float on the water.

The paper clips float because there is something unusual about water's surface. If you could look very, very closely at the surface, you would see the tiny bits or particles that make up water. Each of these tiny particles is called a water molecule. Water molecules are very different from the molecules that make up many other liquids, such as gasoline and alcohol. Water molecules stick together very closely. At the surface, the water molecules stick together so closely that they create a thin layer like a skin. The paper clips cannot break the skin, so they float on top of this layer.

Detergents make it harder for water molecules to stick together to make a thin layer. Without a thin layer to support them, the paper clips sink.

Water also does something unusual when it turns into ice.

Imagine that the water molecules on the surface act like a tissue to hold up the paper clips.

Experiment 7

Getting Bigger

Fill the bottle with water to the very top. Cover the opening of the bottle with a piece of aluminum foil. Place the bottle upright inside the freezer. Wait until the water inside the bottle has completely frozen. What happens to the ice?

Be sure that the bottle is completely filled with water. Also make sure that the foil cap is loose.

When water freezes, the ice takes up more space than the liquid. The ice has no place to go except out through the opening of the bottle. As it squeezes through the opening, it sticks out of the bottle. Usually when a liquid freezes, the solid takes up less space than the liquid. Water is unusual because its solid (ice) takes up more space than its liquid.

Something unusual also happens when ice melts to make water.

Melting Away

You will need:
- cloth towel
- ice cubes
- hammer
- large drinking glass
- thermometer
- paper
- pencil
- lamp with incandescent bulb (optional)
- clock

Wrap the towel around several ice cubes. Ask an adult to crush the ice cubes with the hammer. Fill the glass with water and crushed ice. Place the thermometer inside the glass. Write down the temperature of the ice water. Place the glass in direct sunlight or under a lamp. Every so often, use the thermometer to stir the ice water. Stir gently so that you do not break the thermometer. Every three minutes, write down the temperature. Keep taking the temperature until all the ice has melted. Take five more temperature readings every three minutes.

Notice that the temperature did not go up until most of the ice had melted. The heat from the sun or lamp melted the ice. When all the ice melted, the heat raised the temperature of the water. This is why you see the temperature go up only after most the ice has melted.

The temperature should be about 32 degrees Fahrenheit or about 0 degrees Celsius.

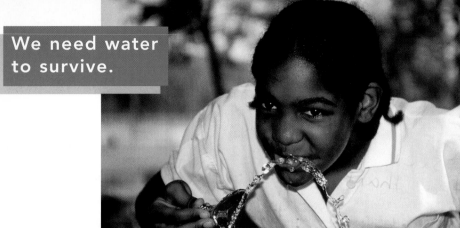

All but one of the pioneers
survived the trip through Death
Valley. Because of the water
cycle, the others survived and
made it to California. Like the
pioneers, we depend on water
for survival. Although water
seems so ordinary, it is really
quite unusual.

Fun With Water

Now that you've learned the importance of water and what makes it so unusual, try this experiment.

You learned that water molecules stick together. See how many drops of water stick together on the top of a penny before the water runs off the coin.

Experiment 9

Counting Drops

Drop the penny into a small glass filled with alcohol. Let the penny soak for a few minutes. The alcohol will clean the penny. Pour off the alcohol. Shake the penny into the paper towel and dry it. Do not touch the penny with your fingers. Use the towel to place the penny on a flat surface. Fill the dropper with water. Hold the dropper straight up and down. Place a drop of water on the penny. Continue placing drops on the

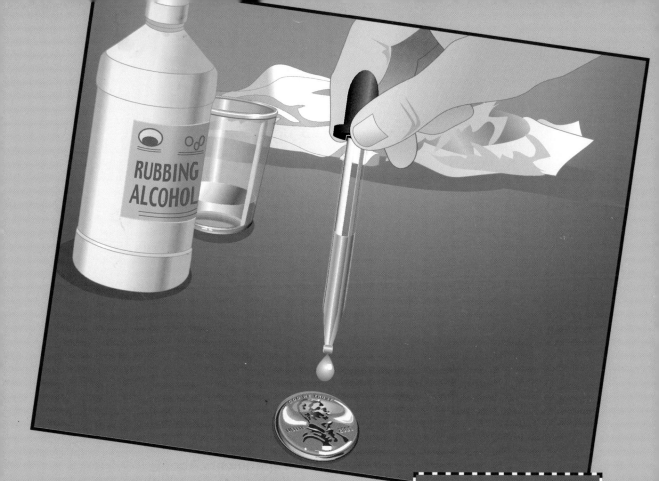

penny, one at a time.
How many drops can you
place on the penny before the
water runs off the coin? Soak
the penny in alcohol and try
again. What is your record?

Because water
molecules stick
together, you
should get more
drops to stay on
the penny than
you might think.

To Find Out More

If you would like to learn more about water, check out these additional resources.

 **Books**

Fiarotta, Noel and Phyllis Fiarotta. **Great Experiments with H₂O.** Sterling Publishers, 1997.

Nankivell-Aston, Sally and Dorothy Jackson. **Science Experiments with Water.** Franklin Watts, 2000.

Perdue, Peggy K. **Diving into Science: Hands-On Water-Related Experiments.** Scott, Foresman and Co., 1990.

Rybolt, Thomas R., and Robert C. Mebane. **Environmental Experiments About Water.** Enslow Publishers, 1993.

VanCleave, Janice Pratt. **Janice VanCleave's Oceans for Every Kid.** John Wiley & Sons, 1996.

Organizations and Online Sites

American Water Works Association

1401 New York Avenue, NW
Suite 640
Washington, DC 20005
202-628-8303
http://www.awwa.org/

This association is a nonprofit group dedicated to improving the quality of drinking water.

Environmental Protection Agency (EPA)

1200 Pennsylvania Avenue, NW
Washington, DC 20460
http://www.epa.gov/ epahome/

The EPA is the United States Government agency in charge of protecting our environment, including the groundwater. Log onto their site and click on "For Kids." You will be led to the Explorers' Club, where you can check out some fun and interesting things to do with water.

The Hands-On Technology Project, Sponsored by Galaxy Network

http://www.galaxy.net/ ~k12/index.shtml/

This site has a number of experiments you can do to learn more about water pollution.

Important Words

displace move something, like water, out of the way

groundwater water that seeps into the ground and becomes a source of drinking water

molecule extremely small particle that makes up water and many other things

precipitation water that falls from the clouds as snow, rain, sleet, or hail

water cycle the passing back and forth of water between Earth and the sky

water vapor what is commonly called steam, but is really a gas

Index

Meet the Author

Salvatore Tocci is a science writer who lives in East Hampton, New York, with his wife, Patti. He was a high school biology and chemistry teacher for almost thirty years. As a teacher, he always encouraged his students to perform experiments in order to learn about and understand science. He loves both sailing and fishing on the water.